PICKING *the* RIGHT COLLEGE

&

FINDING SOME MONEY *to* PAY *for* IT

by:

DAVID G. LANDFAIR

Substantial contribution from:

STEVEN DUCKWORTH

Proofread by:

HEATHER G. WELLS

Edited by:

JOE C. CULPEPPER

Additional copies of this book are available at

Amazon.com

FORWARD

First I must give credit to Steven Duckworth. Steve created a PowerPoint presentation of this material before I ever thought about writing this book. In fact, Steve's presentations were outstanding as he is naturally funny, and the examples he used were personal and heartfelt. Most importantly, however, they got the point across.

I first saw Steve's presentation at Daphne (Ala.) High School. Steve was working at the University of West Florida back then, and his presentation served two purposes. The first was to help high school students pick the right college, and the second was to introduce them to the University of West Florida. This was not a recruiting pitch. It really was something good for the kids, but he was from the University of West Florida so it worked out well for the university too.

Steve's **biggest "take away"** from his presentation was that **"different schools have different rules,"** and he is absolutely correct. Readers, <u>you must contact the university</u> or college you are interested in <u>to find out all "about them, from them."</u> Steve emphasized this point again and again. The reason is that although our friends and families mean well, they do not work for the university. Even the guidance counselors at the high schools may not have the latest information. You can find out the latest from a college or university by calling them. Don't be shy about calling them. That's what they're there for.

Thank you Steve, for giving me permission to use your work in this book to help other people. You are a good man.

TABLE *of* CONTENTS

TABLE *of* CONTENTS *(cont'd)*

Chapter One

INTRODUCTION

Chapter One
INTRODUCTION

The purpose of this book is to help young ladies and gentlemen select the right college and to maximize their chances of receiving some money to help them pay for school as well.

Selecting the right college is very important when you consider that about 28 to 40 percent of freshmen do not return for their sophomore year. You can check the current retention rates by running a quick Internet search. Among the links you will see is one that is a study produced by American College Testing (ACT). **The bottom line is that retention rates matter**, and they should be considered when picking the right the college for you.

I currently teach at Gulf Breeze (Fla.) High School, and I am also an Air Force Admissions Officer. As an Admissions Officer, I interview candidates for admission to the United States Air Force Academy and for Air Force Reserve Officer Training Corps (AFROTC) scholarships. 2012 was by far my busiest year with over 70 interviews. Thirty-three were for the Air Force Academy, some were families who just wanted some guidance, and the rest for ROTC. Sixteen out of the 33 were either appointed to the Air Force Academy or were selected for an Air Force Academy preparatory school, which amounts to an extra year of college for students who need just a little work on a subject or two before starting the rigors of the Academy.

The scholarship interviews resulted in six students receiving scholarships. Two of those students were from Gulf Breeze High School, where our Junior ROTC (JROTC) program had extraordinary success as well. Six seniors asked for help obtaining scholarships, and all six were successful. Two were selected for Air Force ROTC scholarships, two won U.S. Marine Corps ROTC scholarships, one was appointed to West Point (U.S. Army's Academy) and the other to the Air Force Academy.

This unique experience of helping students win scholarships, along with having two daughters in college, has given me an opportunity to learn (sometimes the hard way) about college admissions and scholarship opportunities. **My goal is to pass on those lessons learned in hopes that you will find the right college for you and some money to help pay for it.**

I have been presenting the information in this book to local parents and high school students over the past few years, and I thought that it might be more helpful to have it all written down, rather than parents and students hurriedly taking notes during the presentation.

So here it all is in black and white. I hope it is helpful for you. If it is and the spirit moves you, please feel free to let me know. Now, we must note that as the years pass from the publication date of this book some of the numbers will get stale, but the main concepts will stay the same. Therefore read the numbers as complement to the main concepts and remember, the most important lesson is that **you must take control and you must call the schools you are interested in and find out the latest information yourself**.

THE FAMOUS GOLDEN DOME *of the* UNIVERSITY *of* NOTRE DAME

Chapter Two

FIRST THINGS FIRST

Chapter Two
FIRST THINGS FIRST

Selecting the right college will make all the difference in the world, and there are several things that go into this monumental decision. **The first thing I recommend you do is to make a list of schools.** It does not matter how you pick the schools for this first list. All that matters is that you pick some schools to start with.

You can pick famous football schools, renowned academic schools, schools that are nearby, schools that your parents went to … it does not matter. Just pick some schools. The key thing to remember is that you can always add and delete schools from your list. So I suggest you start with your favorite school. If you don't have one, then pick the biggest and the smallest schools nearby.

In order to make a good comparison, I suggest you include different types of schools. First, put down the local community college and the nearest four-year institution. For us here in Gulf Breeze, Florida, that would be Pensacola State College and the University of West Florida.

Next, put on your list the big "state" schools (state schools are those funded by the state), a big private school in your state, and then add some schools that are located out-of-state but nearby.

So for us here in Gulf Breeze we could put Florida State University, the University of Florida, and the University of Central Florida as some of our big state schools; Miami University as one of our private universities; and we could put the University of South Alabama, the University of Alabama, Auburn University, Louisiana State University, and the University of Georgia as our out-of-state schools.

Now, you might want to add some "others" that interest you. We could add the University of Notre Dame in Indiana, Mississippi State University, and a school that I know a lot about since I used to teach there, the United States Air Force Academy in Colorado.

For starters, our list looks like this:

1.   Pensacola State College (PSC)

2.   University of West Florida (UWF)

3.   Florida State University (FSU)

4.   University of Florida (UF)

5.   University of Central Florida (UCF)

6.   University of Miami (UM)

7.   University of South Alabama (USA)

8.   University of Alabama (UA)

9.   Auburn University (AU)

10.   Louisiana State University (LSU)

11.   University of Georgia (UG)

12.   University of Notre Dame (ND)

13.   Mississippi State University (MSU)

14.   United States Air Force Academy (USAFA)

Wow! We already have fourteen schools that we are looking at, and we hardly even tried. That's great! Remember, you can add and delete as you go. You can add schools from the all over the country. Next thing we need to do is to start narrowing this list or adding to it if we see something better or are just curious about another choice.

Chapter Three

NARROWING YOUR CHOICES – STANDARDIZED TESTS

Chapter Three
NARROWING YOUR CHOICES – STANDARDIZED TESTS

As an Air Force Admissions Officer, I get calls all the time about what it takes to get into the U.S. Air Force Academy (USAFA) or to get an Air Force ROTC scholarship. The first thing I always tell them is: To pass through the first door you have to walk through requires **a qualifying ACT (American College Test) score or SAT (Scholastic Aptitude Test) score.** (This applies to almost every school.)

In response, parents and students often ask, "Why do schools rely so much on the ACT or SAT score when a person's grade point average (GPA) is such a good indicator of success?"

I explain that the problem is there really is no way of telling whether Mr. Jones' English class in Florida is just as difficult or as easy as Mrs. Smith's English class in Arizona. ACT and SAT tests are standardized; they are the same for everyone. So although GPAs tend to be an indicator of success, ACT and SAT scores offer a uniform measure to compare students' knowledge on a set of academic subjects.

Please do not take away that GPAs do not matter. They do matter, but the standardized tests count more at many schools. GPAs matter for many other things. For example, many scholarships are based on your GPA, and a lot of sororities and fraternities use GPAs during the recruitment process.

The next question I often receive is about advanced placement classes, typically called AP classes and honor classes. What about those, and how do they count?

This is a good question and where **"different schools have different rules"** comes into play. To learn and understand these differentiating rules, you must call the admissions offices of the schools to which you are applying and specifically ask about the weight given to these classes.

I know at USAFA, the admissions board considers AP classes and honor classes, but I do not know how much of a consideration they get. I would bet almost all colleges are the same way. The biggest thing these classes show is that the student took the most challenging classes available. That is important.

I do remember asking the question myself when I toured Florida State University and the University of Florida with my daughters. The school recruiting representatives recommended "you should have at least three to six AP or honors courses." So the final answer to that question is the weight given those classes depends on the school you are applying to, but since some sort of consideration for undertaking (and hopefully doing well in) the most challenging classes available must be given, take them!

The bottom line is that for almost every school, the ACT and/or the SAT is the predominant factor of the selection process.

Here is what I recommend: Inquire directly to the school and ask, "What was the mean ACT or SAT score of the freshman class last year?"

ACT scores are evaluated by the Composite Score (the average of the four individual tests –English, Mathematics, Reading, Science) and each subject test separately. Each test score and the Composite Score range from 1 (low) to 36 (high).

SAT scores are reported on a scale from 200-800, with additional subscores reported for the essay (ranging from 2-12) and for multiple-choice writing questions (on a 20-80 scale).

The mean ACT score for the freshman class at USAFA is usually about 29 or 30. So when a student asks me what it takes to get into USAFA, I tell them that they must have an "exceptional" score and that the board "looks at other things as well."

One scenario goes something like this. If they are a high school senior and have a top score of 20, I tell them that their chances are slim and that they have a long road to go if they are going to make it and should probably look elsewhere. If they are high school junior with a 25, I tell them to get some tutoring, take the test again and their score probably will go up, which could make them competitive.

In summary, you need to find out what the mean ACT and SAT scores of the freshman class are at the schools on your list, and then you can work from there.

Since this is such an important point, let's look at an example by looking up the scores posted for freshman admission 2013 for each of our listed schools. I did this with a simple Internet search on each school's site.

1.   Pensacola State College (PSC) – Open Admission Policy means the ACT/SAT score is not a real consideration

2.   University of West Florida (UWF) – 22

3.   Florida State University (FSU) – 27

4.   University of Florida (UF) – 29

5.   University of Central Florida (UCF) – 27

6.   University of Miami (UM) – 30

7.   University of South Alabama (USA) – 22

8.   University of Alabama (UA) – 25

9.   Auburn University (AU) – 27

10.   Louisiana State University (LSU) – 22

11.   University of Georgia (UG) - 28

12.   University of Notre Dame (ND) – 30

13.   Mississippi State University (MSU) – 23

14.   United States Air Force Academy (USAFA) - 30

After looking at this data, one can conclude a couple of things. First, you need to see if your ACT score is below, at, or above the average freshman at the school you want to attend. If, for example, I am a high school junior with a 20 on my ACT and I want to attend the University of Georgia, I am significantly below the average score being reported at 28. As a junior, I have time to take the ACT again and to get some tutoring to bring up my score. I may have a chance to get my score up to 28, but I probably should also be looking at another school just in case.

The question to ask yourself before fighting your way to a higher ACT score – Is the score indicative of your academic knowledge and ability to apply that knowledge or was it just the result of a series of bad test days? If the school is asking for a high score, it is certain that the classes you will take there will be rigorous. Duckworth used to talk about this during his presentation, and he was absolutely correct. He used to say that if you did get into your school of choice but your **ACT score was below the mean, you may struggle and not be happy.**

Please do not pass by the point above without taking note of it. This is very important.

To continue with our example, let's say our junior received some tutoring and improved his ACT score from 20 to 25, and he was accepted at the University of Georgia where the average score for a freshman is 28. (The reason this would be possible is that the mean is an average – there will be some scores below and some above that number.) Statistics show that even though our student did get accepted with that below average score, it is then likely he that he may continue to be a below average student.

Let's put it this way and it will be clearer. Maybe it would be better if the student with a 25 on his ACT went to Louisiana State University instead, where the mean score is 22. Then he might be an above average student, where good grades come a bit easier and his life is a good bit better.

I don't know about you, but I do remember that getting good grades made me and my financiers (my parents) happy, and when I was happy I got better grades.

Remember this when we talk later about scholarships in Chapter Eleven because continuing scholarships (scholarships that pay every year) usually require good grades in order to keep them.

Considering again that statistic that some 28 to 40 percent of freshmen do not return for their sophomore year, finding a school that fits you academically is very important. Remember that different schools have different rules, and find the mean ACT/SAT score of freshman class at the school you want to go to so that you can make sure you fit in.

UNIVERSITY *of* FLORIDA'S SMALL ANIMAL HOSPITAL

Chapter Four

NARROWING YOUR CHOICES –
WITH THE END IN MIND

Chapter Four
NARROWING YOUR CHOICES –
WITH THE END IN MIND

We can start narrowing down our choices by looking at our list of schools with different colored glasses. What I mean here is that each school is going to present different pros and cons during the selection process depending on how we look at them.

One set of glasses you may want to use to narrow down your long list of schools is a pair that filters out everything except what you want to do in life. In other words, **we can start with the end in mind – the real purpose of why you are going to be there**. For example, if you want to become a teacher, then you probably should pick a university that offers a degree in education. It becomes more difficult if you want to become part of a profession that requires even higher education, like becoming a doctor or a lawyer. If you want to become a veterinarian, for example, then you may want to go to a school that has that type of graduate school.

My Daughter's Experience

Here is an example from personal experience. One of my daughters wanted to become a veterinarian, so our initial step was to find out what you have to do to become a veterinarian. We found that first you must get your undergraduate degree, then you go back to school for your graduate degree in veterinarian medicine.

Our second step was to look for universities that had graduate schools offering degrees in veterinarian medicine, and we found that there are only a few. In fact, there are about one per state. The schools closest to us are UF, LSU, Georgia, Auburn and MSU.

Our third step was to visit them all the summer between my daughter's junior and senior years and ask them what it takes to get selected to their graduate school. What we found out was that they all have an unwritten rule, that makes absolutely all the sense in the world – *you have a better chance of getting selected to their graduate school if you go to their undergraduate school.*

Before we started our journey to visit these schools, we thought that a person could get an undergraduate degree anywhere and then apply to a graduate school and get in. It can be done, but the odds are not great.

Here is what one school representative said: "Put it this way, Mr. Landfair. We will have 60 open desks next year in our graduate school. It is pretty likely that about 50 of those desks will be filled with students who have their undergraduate degree from here." She did not have to say any more than that. If you are at the top of your class when you are an undergraduate from an unaffiliated school, you will be competitive, but you might want to hedge your bet and get your undergraduate degree from the school that also offers your graduate program.

Now I must say that I do not know if this is true with all types of graduate schools. I am just telling you our experience with veterinarian schools. **The lesson learned** is that if in the end you want to go to graduate school, my advice is for you to go and **talk to that school in person**. Get a tour and ask them what they are looking for when you apply for admission. You may find out that it is a different story, and then again, you may not.

So as a result of our experience, our list shrunk from fourteen to five schools. We were now looking at UF, LSU, Georgia, Auburn and MSU. We visited each one to "try them out for size."

Chapter Five

TRY THEM OUT FOR SIZE

Chapter Five
TRY THEM OUT FOR SIZE

I **highly recommend** that you visit the schools you are really serious about attending. You are about to spend four years at this school, and you want to succeed while you are there. If you don't like where you are, then you might not succeed.

That terrible statistic that states that some 28 to 40 percent of freshmen do not return for their sophomore year has to be decreased. One way to do it is to check out the school you want to go to firsthand, so you can make sure you are comfortable there.

A high school classmate of mine is now an Associate Dean in the Engineering School at the University of Alabama. His name is Chuck Carr, and he returned to Gulf Breeze High School one day to talk to students who had UA on their list. The **advice** that he gave the students was right on the mark. He said that you need to try the school on for size. He said that you will discover *"one size does not necessarily fit all,"* and that you will know when you visit the campus if that school is for you.

My Daughter's Experience

When my daughter and I visited MSU, I was really impressed. I thought it would be a great fit. I also liked that the tuition was less for their graduate school. So I was excited! My daughter, on the other hand, just did not "feel it." She didn't like the campus layout very well and just didn't feel like the school fit her.

The University of Georgia was the same way. We really liked their tour. It was very well done and professional. The softball program even invited her to walk on and play for them, but she didn't feel that school fit her either.

Our visit to the University of Florida was a home run. Although I played football at FSU, and we feel some loyalty there, she felt like

UF and the veterinarian school there fit her. I liked the fact that she could use her Bright Futures scholarship there, and that helped her make the decision. We will talk more about the money angle in the next chapter.

My Experience

I remember my own experience. I was recruited out of Gulf Breeze High to play football at the United States Merchant Marine Academy (USMMA) in Kings Point, New York. They flew me up there to check it out and laid out the red carpet. I only visited one other college, UA, and really that was to go to a football game with some friends. I liked UA and thought the football program at USMMA looked worse than my high school program. I actually thought I would be stepping down. It didn't feel like a good fit, but guess what? Although I had scholarship offers from other schools, I accepted the "full ride" from USMMA and then transferred after the football season was over.

Money is a huge factor in deciding on your education, and scholarships can vary as widely as the schools that offer them. USMMA is one of five federally funded academies. The other four are: the U.S. Military Academy in West Point, New York; the U.S. Naval Academy in Annapolis, Maryland; the Air Force Academy in Colorado Springs, Colorado; and the Coast Guard Academy in New London, Connecticut. All of these schools are "full rides." All (or just about all) expenses are paid.

In fact, as an Air Force Admissions Officer, I go to local area schools and award appointments to the Air Force Academy. In my speech, I say that the appointment is valued at about $400,000. So when I left USMMA, I left a huge scholarship behind and suddenly had no scholarships to pay for school. I was lucky. I had saved a little money over the years, and my parents were able to fund my education at Florida State University since I still qualified for "in-state" tuition.

So a good fit can make all the difference in your educational experience and by consequence your subsequent career, but let's face it, a huge part of the decision process is cost. If you don't have the money or can't get the money, the "fit" is moot. I gave up a huge scholarship. My daughter chose to go to UF because that school felt like it was a better fit for her; but, honestly, it was a better fit monetarily as well.

Chapter Six

THE MONEY ANGLE

Chapter Six
THE MONEY ANGLE

Money matters, and money will affect most people's selection process a lot! Let's take another set of glasses and filter out everything else in the college selection process but the money.

There are several costs to consider. Among them are tuition, books, fees, room and board, entertainment and transportation. Let's take our list and start comparing costs.

Tuition is huge, and it varies from school to school. It is usually quoted as "per credit hour," but not always. As I mentioned previously, **different schools have different rules** and that is certainly true when it comes to tuition and the other costs as well.

I **recommend** that you go to the Internet site of each school to find the various costs. I **highly recommend** that you do not use any sources not authorized by the school for this task because you need to compare apples to apples, so you don't end up with false data, throwing your comparison off.

For our example, I used the webpage of each school to look up the tuition and fees per credit hour for both in-state students (students who meet residency requirements for that school) and out-of-state students. Again, this was a little difficult because the schools' sites state their charges differently, but being official sources, I could trust the numbers would be current and good ones.

The following are the results of my "tuition information" searches for each of the fourteen schools on our original list (remember, these searches were done in 2013).

My recommendation is to call the school you are interested in and get the information you need straight from them.

TUITION RATES

1. PSC – $120 In-State and $486 Out-of-State

2. UWF - $207 In-State and $637 Out-of-State

3. FSU - $212 In-State and $717 Out-of-State

4. UF- $204 In-State and $ 947 Out-of-State

5. UCF -$208 In-State and $744 Out-of-State

6. UM - $2,366 (Private School)

7. USA – $277 In-State and $554 Out-of-State

8. UA - $295 In-State and $748 Out-of-State

9. Auburn -$328 In-State and $984 Out-of-State

10. LSU - $259 In-State and $856 Out-of-State

11. Georgia – $641 In-State and $1,779 Out-of-State

12. ND -$1,486 (Private School)

13. MSU - $391 In-State and $987 Out-of-State

14. USAFA – No Charge at any of the Federal Academies

If you are looking for a fast overview comparison, you can find sites on the Internet that will compare prices for you. Collegecost.ed.gov is run by the U.S. Department of Education. It may work for you. It's definitely worth a try, as long as you keep in mind that the information may not be current and may not be directly from the school, so don't use its data as final numbers when calculating what you will actually pay. Again, **my advice** is when your list gets down to just a few schools, contact those schools and find out exactly what the costs are from them.

Unfortunately, there is more to pay than just tuition and fees. One of the biggest costs besides tuition is room and board. Living in a dormitory (dorm) is an option, or you can get an apartment and share it with friends. By far the least expensive way is to stay home. I can just hear you say "No Way!" (both kids and parents), but this may be a really good deal for many.

PUGH HALL *at the* UNIVERSITY *of* FLORIDA

Consider this line of thinking. When you graduate from college, **the only thing that really matters is where you graduated from**. In other words, the last school you attended. So you may want to think about staying at home and attending the local community college your first two years of college before transferring to the school you want to graduate from. For us, that is Pensacola State College, and then you could transfer to the University of Florida or some other college or university. Many community colleges have agreements with universities for guaranteed transfers, making this route a literal shoo-in to your preferred school at a bargain price. If you choose this path, make sure to call the school you are looking to

31

graduate from and ask if such an agreement with the local community college exists and what the requirements are to transfer.

Whichever way you choose to go, call the university and find out how much it costs to live in the dorm and explore every possible living situation you can think of and all the accompanying fees and costs so you are not caught paying double. Here is what happened to my youngest daughter.

My Daughter's Experience

When my youngest daughter found out that she was accepted to Florida State University, we were all excited. It was recommended that we sign up for a dorm as soon as possible, so we did at the very hour the applications opened up online.

She ended up with a dorm that required a meal plan. That was all fine and good, until she got into a sorority. The fees for the sorority also included meals, so now we were paying for meals TWICE. The good news is that the school offered a discounted meal plan; conversely, it was still not a significant discount, and it was still required.

In the end, we paid for a lot of meals our daughter never ate. The **lesson learned** was to be prepared for unanticipated and potentially duplicate fees. There were other dorms available that did not have the meal plan requirement, but those dorms were not in the middle of campus and did not have the other options my daughter desired. As a result, we paid "in meals" for the convenience of getting the dorm she really liked.

Other costs include books and entertainment. The deal with books are different from school to school. Here again, Duckworth's warning "different schools have different rules" holds true. Both my daughters (one at UF and the other at FSU) buy books differently. My daughter at FSU gets her books online, while my daughter at UF goes to the bookstore on campus. One rents her books, and the other sells her books back at the end of the semester.

Here is what I learned when I wrote my textbook as an Associate Professor at the Air Force Academy. I was a Course Director, and my class was required for all juniors. More than 1,000 students took that class every year. The book company was guaranteed that at least 1,000 books would be sold every time we changed texts. They, of course, liked that and encouraged us to change texts as often as we desired.

Some schools have lucrative contracts with publishers and are encouraged to publish. Other schools use what is already available on the market. The **bottom line** is that textbooks are big business in the publishing world, so whether you buy or rent your texts, it will be a significant expense.

My daughters' bills range from $100 to nearly $700 for books each semester – as I said, a significant expense. It is something you will have to budget for no matter what school you attend.

Entertainment needs to be budgeted for as well. Some schools impose a mandatory fee that entitles students to obtain discounted or free tickets to football and basketball games and other extracurricular activities. Football is really big at some schools, and the tempo at the school is dictated by the football schedule. Other schools are affected more by basketball. Regardless, many students go to the games and are swept up in the revelry. This, of course, is not free and therefore becomes another line item on your budget.

Lastly, don't forget to budget for personal items such as doing the laundry. Many Laundromats eat quarters like crazy. I know, it sounds absurd to worry about quarters in the face of tuition, books and room and board, but quarters add up and laundry, for your own sake and all those you live and go to school with, should be done often. Check out what the laundry facilities are at or near the places you are considering to live.

CHIEF OSCEOLA *and* RENEGADE *at* FLORIDA STATE UNIVERSITY

Chapter Seven

BIG OR SMALL DISTRACTIONS

Chapter Seven
BIG OR SMALL DISTRACTIONS

Another thing to consider is the environment that will best serve you. Remember that frightening statistic, some 28 to 40 percent of freshmen do not return for their sophomore year. There are many reasons why.

We have already talked about academic difficulty in Chapter Three, but this is worth repeating here because the "difficulty" creates part of the environment that you will either thrive in or only hope to endure. If you are able to get into a school whose freshman class average is a 25 on the ACT and you have a 23, then you may struggle to keep up academically. You may want to go to a school where you have a better-than-average ACT score. If, for example, you have a 23 on your ACT, you may want to go to a school where the freshman class average is a 22. You may excel at that school, and that might make all the difference in continuing into and through the following three years. It is worth thinking about.

A FOOTBALL WEEKEND *at* FLORIDA STATE UNIVERSITY

One thing to consider is how large the school is. Why? Big schools usually have big distractions. Big football schools have big stadiums that fill up during game day with multitudes of fans.

Many of them are there to party and have a good time. This type of atmosphere throughout the fall can prove to be a big distraction.

Many of these schools have big basketball, soccer and baseball programs as well. The distractions go on all year long. Then there are the schools located close to the beach and those located close to the slopes (skiing).

Speaking of big schools, I remember feeling a bit like a number when I was at Florida State. I registered for classes with my student number. I paid for classes with that number, and I got my grades with that number. I really felt that I was just a number to the university.

To add to it, in many classes I had no clue who my professor was because the class was so big I couldn't see his face on the stage below. The same can be true for online classes, where interaction between the student and the professor or other students may not be required or encouraged.

ALMOST 100,000 *at* UNIVERSITY *of* ALABAMA FOOTBALL GAME

The nice thing about smaller schools is that they usually offer smaller classes, where you have access to the professor. When I taught at the Air Force Academy, my largest class was a little over 20 students. I offered tutoring in the afternoons and evenings. In my case, the students received tutoring from the same person who was responsible for the text and the course learning objectives. I wrote them. It was easy for me to explain what I wanted the students to walk away with.

Juxtapose this with my economics class at Florida State when I was an undergrad which was taught in a three-level auditorium. I remember trying to make an appointment to see the professor. It turned out to be a graduate assistant, and the line was an hour long.

Instead, I asked an old classmate from high school for help. I ended up with a good grade in that class, but my experience was as different as night from day to what is offered at the Air Force Academy and many other smaller schools.

Let's take a look at the enrollment of the schools on our list:

1.   Pensacola State College (PSC) – 36,000

2.   University of West Florida (UWF) – 13,000

3.   Florida State University (FSU) – 41,000

4.   University of Florida (UF) – 50,000

5.   University of Central Florida (UCF) – 59,000

6.   University of Miami (UM) – 15,000

7.   University of South Alabama (USA) – 15,000

8.   University of Alabama (UA) – 33,000

9.   Auburn University (AU) – 25,000

10.   Louisiana State University (LSU) – 30,000

11.   University of Georgia – (UG) 34,000

12.   University of Notre Dame (ND) – 11,000

13.   Mississippi State University (MSU) – 20,000

14.   United States Air Force Academy (USAFA) – 4,000

The **bottom line** is that big schools offer big distractions and less access to your professors. When you talk to the admissions officers of the universities on your list, ask them about class size. It will make a difference in your college experience.

PENSACOLA STATE COLLEGE NOW OFFERS *a* FEW FOUR-YEAR DEGREES

Chapter Eight

WHERE IS EVERYONE ELSE GOING?

Chapter Eight
WHERE IS EVERYONE ELSE GOING?

One question that may be on your mind at this point is "where is everyone else going?" It's a good question, and I can tell you here at Gulf Breeze High School - a school that routinely scores as one of the better schools in the State of Florida - the statistics tell an interesting story.

Before I start, the statistics have to be taken with a grain of salt. They are from the school newspaper, which gets some of its information directly from the students, some from our guidance department, and some, I am sure, from the rumor mill. Having said that, statistics are an indicator, and they are worth a look.

The two years I have data for show first that each graduating class had over 360 graduates. Nearly half, 47 percent, chose to go to a local college (the University of West Florida and Pensacola State College, which is the local community college). I expect many did so because it is a less expensive option to stay local or "in-state," as discussed in Chapter Six.

Nearly 60 percent of those students (that's 60% of the 47% mentioned in the previous paragraph) chose Pensacola State. Another factor may have been that Pensacola State College has an open admissions policy, as mentioned in Chapter Three.

Money and qualifying admissions scores are common deciding factors, but there is another that can be devastating – missed deadlines. It is very important to start your research early so you can apply not only to the schools you want most to attend, but apply for scholarships as well. As we discussed in Chapter Six, it can be an excellent idea to save money by getting your Associates Degree at the local college and then transferring to a four-year institution, but this route should be your chosen path, not the path left to you because of a missed deadline.

Including the students who chose to stay local, a little more than 60 percent stayed "in-state." After looking at the "out-of-state" tuition rates in Chapter Six, this does not surprise me at all.

About 15 percent decided to go to the two big state universities (Florida State University and the University of Florida). It is very **interesting to note** that all but two or three of that 15 percent were Honor Graduates. (Honor Graduate status was bestowed for achieving a 94-percent weighted grade point average or higher. I read the honor graduate information in the Graduation Program at commencement.)

THE UNIVERSITY *of* WEST FLORIDA *in* PENSACOLA

A little more than 15 percent chose schools that charged out-of-state tuition. I make a distinction here by saying "out-of-state tuition," because some colleges will waive or give scholarships to cancel out the "out-of-state" price hike. For example, the last time I talked to the admissions office at the University of South Alabama (located about an hour from Gulf Breeze, Florida), they said they had a waiver for students in our county and the neighboring county.

I understand this is a common practice, and I **highly recommend** that you check this out at the schools you are interested in attending. Ask admissions if they have a waiver for the "out-of-state" fee or what it would take to qualify for a scholarship that pays the "out-of-state" fee.

The bottom line is that the statistics show that most students stayed "in-state," most likely because of the "out-of-state" tuition hike. The data also shows that nearly half of our graduates chose either the local community college (Pensacola State College) or the University of West Florida.

Chapter Nine

BEFORE YOU PICK YOUR SCHOOL, CONTACT THEM

Chapter Nine
BEFORE YOU PICK YOUR SCHOOL, CONTACT THEM

Before we start the chapter on Picking the Right College, I want to review a couple of points. In the "Forward," I told you of Steve Duckworth's driving point: **"Different Schools Have Different Rules."** It is true with regard to every topic we've covered – admissions requirements, class sizes, costs and fees…. This is why I want to encourage you to contact the schools you have on your list. Find out what their rules are, their application process, and their timetables.

Take the opportunity to make contacts at your school, the local community college or community center when they host a **college fair**. Go armed with your list of schools and questions, ready to gather information.

In fact, maybe you should go ahead and make a table! On the top of each table, write the name of one of your schools, then along the left-hand side put in the questions you want to ask.

Now you might want to do your research first, so you can fill in the information you could not find yourself, or you can simply try to get as much as you can when you see them. I would recommend the former rather than the later, since then you can confirm with the school representatives what you have learned through your initial searches. This also serves to make a good first impression with the school representatives, to whom you will seem better prepared than many they will see on a fair day. Remember to bring extra pencils & pens!

Your table might look something like the following example (and you can use the back of the pages for additional notes).

University of Florida	
What is the mean ACT/SAT score of your freshmen class this year and what is the retention rate of freshmen at your school?	
Do you have my major, and are there any special requirements to be selected for admission to your school? **NOTE:** *Many schools have prerequisites.*	
How big is your school and what is the average size of a class? How many students commute, and how many live on campus?	
Do you have a graduate program in my subject and is there preference in admittance for having earned an undergraduate degree here?	
What is the Admission Board looking for? *For example,* 1) Do I get any extra points for being a legacy (mom or dad went to school there), or if I am the first in my family to go to college? 2) Do I get extra points for completing four years of a foreign language or for taking some other special class? 3) Is there an essay required? If so, is it used for everyone or is it used as a tie-breaker?	

University of Florida

What is your application deadline and when does your application become available?	
Can out-of-state tuition fees be waived?	
Do you "superscore" ACT or SAT scores? (see Chapt 10)	
Do you have any special scholarships that I qualify for ... *(add to the rest of this sentence ... for example, I am the President of our Student Government Association)*?	
How much is the "total" cost to go your school? They will typically give you a brochure listing their costs. Before you leave, **READ IT** when you get a chance so you can go back and ask questions if needed.	
Contact information – get their business card, or if they don't have one, ask for their information in case you have more questions later.	
When do you recommend I submit my application, and what affect might that have on getting into a dormitory?	

My Experience at the College Fair

I **highly recommend** going to the college fair, especially the one at your school if they have one. When I was 18 and a senior at Gulf Breeze High, I went to the college fair. I had no plan, no guidance, and really no idea what was going on. I had taken the ACT and the SAT, so that was good. I even knew my scores, but I did not know what to do with them (like ask the college representatives what the mean score was for the freshman class at their institution).

I did not collect literature. I just looked around (*please, do not let this be you*). I think the only reason I was there was because I was the president of the Student Government Association and was supposed to be there to help host the event.

Fortunately for me, Charles Gray, the Dean of the high school at that time, introduced me to the representative from Mississippi College. Gray said that I was captain of both our championship baseball team and our winning football team. He said I got good grades and was the president of the Student Government Association.

The representative asked me if I knew about Mississippi College (in Clinton, Miss.), and I confessed that I did not. He told me about the school and then asked if I wanted to play football for them if they gave me a scholarship. I told him the truth – I had thought about playing football in college but I didn't want my tuition to be connected to playing ball, because I wasn't sure my body could hold up to that level of bruising. (Funny thing is, I ended up playing at Florida State for a short time, and I was knocked unconscious during a tackling drill which ended up being my last play in college.)

The representative repeated his football question several times and finally asked me to think about it. I told him I honestly did not know much about his school, so I wasn't prepared to accept his offer, and I really didn't want to play football to pay my bills.

He said: "How about if we give you all of what I offered, and all you have to do is go to school? You don't have to play football."

MISSISSIPPI COLLEGE

I asked him what he meant, and he said the offer was really a leadership scholarship. All I had to do is enroll in the school and there would be no strings attached, except that I needed to get good grades. Again, he told me to think about it.

I was very happy that someone took interest in me, but I wasn't prepared for this conversation, mainly because I had never heard of the school and I left saying, "No, thank you."

The **lesson learned** here is that you should _**be prepared when you go to the college fair**_. Don't just go to the fair to pick up literature. Go ready to ask questions (consider using the table from this chapter) and see what they offer. Ask about scholarships. Make contacts so you can call them later to find out more information or to verify information you come across later.

Chapter Ten

PICKING THE RIGHT COLLEGE

Chapter Ten
PICKING THE RIGHT COLLEGE

As you narrow down your list, don't forget that you need to always have a "Plan B." The reason is that getting into college is not easy, and getting into some schools is like winning the lottery. The following statistics give you an idea of how difficult it really is to get selected.

2013 SEARCH				
	UF	USAFA	FSU	UWF
Mean ACT – of Freshman Class	29	30	27	22
# of Applicants	27,295	12,732	28,313	5,744
% Offered Admission	43%	9%	58%	63%
Freshman Class Size	6,742	1,071	6,774	1,460

As you can see, it is a good idea to apply to more than one school. When I sit down with candidates to the Air Force Academy for their interviews, I always remind them to have a "Plan B," because the responses they get may be unexpected or even unfair. They may feel they are qualified, or perhaps over qualified, but are not picked for admission. If, however, they have applied to several, they may be selected by a different school. So **my advice** is to apply to as many as you can. Your odds go up with the number you apply to, and, if you are accepted to more than one, then you will have the enviable pleasure of deciding which is the best fit for you.

A note about the above statistics. You should keep in mind when you look at these statistics that there were thousands that applied who really had no hope of getting in. They did not look at the prerequisites and were out before they even started. ***Do not let this be you.*** YES, apply to several, but only to those whose requirements you meet. So don't, for example, apply to the University of Florida when your best score on the ACT is a 19. You will not get in. You may get into the University of West Florida because 19 is a lot closer to the freshmen class average of 22.

LEVIN LAW SCHOOL *at the* UNIVERSITY *of* FLORIDA

Again, go to the college fairs! Ask the school representatives what they are looking for. Ask them all the questions on your table. If you cannot go to the fair, CALL! Remember, **different schools have different rules**. Call every one of the schools you are interested in and ask all the questions you've thought of, then start comparing them.

When you ask what ACT or SAT score they are looking for, ask if they **superscore**. Superscoring is when only the best segments of all of your scores are used. For example, let's say you received a 22 on the math part of the ACT and a 24 on the verbal, which makes your composite score a 23 for the first set of tests. The second time you took the test, you did better in one segment and a little worse in the other – a 26 on the verbal but a 21 on the math. Your **superscore** would be the combined best of those two testing attempts – so a 22 on the math and a 26 on verbal gives you a higher composite score of 24.

Ask how many advanced placement (AP) or honor courses they are looking for, and if they give points for community service hours. Ask them if they have a requirement for an essay and how much it counts.

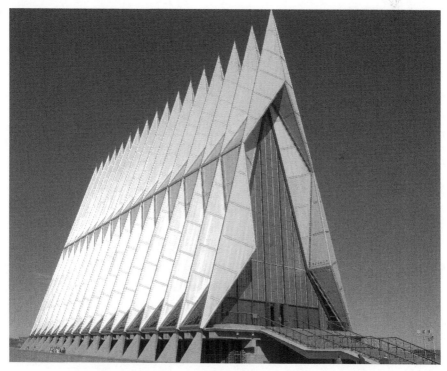

THE CHAPEL *at the* UNITED STATES AIR FORCE ACADEMY

One admissions officer at a really big school told me that the essay was only used as a tie-breaker at his school, so very few essays are actually read. Another admissions officer at a different school said that the essays count a lot. I know at the Air Force Academy they count, so you have to do your best. **My recommendation** is to get help when you write your essays; make sure to use spellcheck; have someone else read it – it's too easy to miss something when you have spent a long time writing a paper because your mind knows what it wants to say and will fill it in when you are reading the paper back to yourself even though the words aren't actually on the page. Strange, but true.

Ask if you get extra points for taking a second language.

Ask whether special consideration is given for being a legacy (a child or grandchild of a graduate from that school), or for being the first from your family to go to college, or for being a member of a minority.

As you are filling out your tables, discard those schools with requirements you do not meet. This will save you money on application fees! And speaking of which, remember money drives most of the decision, so make sure to include schools you can afford without the help of scholarships or grants, in case you do not win those you apply for and do not qualify for financial aid.

Narrowing the field. Let's build a matrix to help visualize this. Since ACT scores and money are usually the deciding factors, a matrix of just these facts for your remaining schools may be the best way to see in a single shot the data that will help you decide which schools you will next discard. The matrix on the upcoming page is composed of 6 columns: (1) my remaining schools, (2) the mean ACT score of the freshman class last year, (3) tuition, (4) housing costs, (5) scholarships (this is a big one and can make all the difference), and (6) my ranking.

THE STUDENT SECTION IS FULL *at* FLORIDA STATE UNIVERSITY

Take a look and see how you would rank these schools if you had a 26 on your ACT, qualified for a Florida's Bright Futures Medallion Scholarship (which pays nearly 80 percent of your tuition cost), and had little other money to help pay the bills.

2013 STATISTICS					
SCHOOL	MEAN ACT SCORE	TUITION	HOUSING	SCHOLARSHIPS	MY RANKING
FSU	27	$ 5,238	$ 5,280	Bright Futures	3
UWF	22	$ 3,016	$ 0 *Stay at home*	Bright Futures	1
USA	22	$ 3,690 *in-state* $ 7,202 *out*	$ 1,610	Out-of-State Tuition Waiver	2
MSU	23	$ 5,805 *in-state* $ 14,670 *out*	$ 4,612	Out-of-State Tuition Scholarship	4

With a 26 on the ACT, you look good academically at all these schools, except at FSU where you are a tad below the mean. This is not a big deal. You are not far below, so you should be okay academically, but academics will not be a piece of cake either. You may have to work harder at this school than the others. At the other three schools, your score is above average, so not only may you not struggle academically, you may excel.

Let's say you also visited them all, and you liked all four. Which one would you pick?

At this point, it may come down to money. Let's look first at tuition. If you use the Florida Bright Futures scholarship, your tuition fees at both FSU and UWF would be less than USA and MSU, but that really is to be expected since they will be charging out-of-state tuition. Ah, but wait, remember that **different schools have different rules**, and USA waives out-of-state tuition for Escambia and Santa Rosa County, Florida residents.

Mississippi State offers an out-of-state tuition scholarship for students who achieve a certain score on their ACT. (The last time I checked that was a 26 ACT score, but that number could change so call them if you are interested.)

Now we can look at room and board. Of course the least expensive option is to stay at home. If you have that option, then you have a big decision to make. If that is your decision, UWF is the ticket, and remember academically your 26 on the ACT shows that you probably will be an above-average student as well.

NOTE: The numbers used in the preceding matrix will change. We are using them as an exercise in narrowing and ultimately deciding on a school. When you make your matrix with your remaining schools, make sure your numbers are the most current and gathered from the schools themselves. Investigate what kind of scholarships or tuition waivers are available so you can add them to your matrix as well. The **bottom line** is that your decision matrix can make quick work of narrowing down the final candidate schools, if not showing you an "obvious choice."

Chapter Eleven

FINDING MONEY TO HELP PAY THE BILLS

Chapter Eleven
FINDING MONEY TO HELP PAY THE BILLS

Let's be honest, even if you have the scores to get into the school of your dreams, if the money isn't there you won't be able to go. That is why I encourage people to start looking early and often for scholarships and grants.

First, money is money. The more you can get of it, the better off you will be. So **I highly encourage students to apply for as many scholarships as possible, _even if they are small_.** Several small scholarships add up.

My Daughter's Experience

My daughter applied for several small scholarships and won a few. They were not big, but when we added it all up, she had enough money to pay to join a sorority at FSU.

The first one she pursued was the Veterans of Foreign Wars audio/essay contest where she had to write an essay on patriotism and then record it. She sent it in and won $250. Then she entered an essay contest with the local Optimist Club and won $300. She entered a few more and never heard back. She entered some big-name scholarship contests with Coca-Cola and Best Buy, and she won one for $1,500. All total, she won over $2,000 to spend her freshman year in college.

You may not win when you enter these contests and competitions, but **you can't win if you don't enter**. Enter as many as you can – it may end up to be worth all the effort.

Now to optimize your chances, **my advice** is to look out for the "low-hanging fruit" and snatch it up before someone else does. My experience is that a lot of this fruit is advertised at schools and within the community. The schools are even asked to recommend students for some of these scholarships. Find out what scholarships your school is advertising, how they advertise them (in case new ones are posted), and if they have been asked to recommend students for any of the scholarships. Then apply to all that you are eligible for.

At Gulf Breeze High, the guidance office posts the scholarships and their deadlines, and they get advertised during announcements. Sadly, I have seen quite a few get re-advertised or re-emphasized because no one applied for them. I have seen several go to the only person who applied. <u>Make these the first scholarships you pursue</u>.

My bet is that there are three reasons why some scholarships are not applied for. One is that for some scholarships' requirements are so high or exhaustive, only a few people are eligible or willing to put in that much effort, so that makes sense. Another is that people must not be hearing about them, so those scholarships go untapped. My third guess is that people are not applying because they don't think they can win, perhaps because they believe the pool of applicants is too great. Well, since we know very few are applying for the smaller and more obscure scholarships, mathematically your chances are way up. The **bottom line** is that there are LOTS of scholarships and grants being offered. Find them at your school and online, then apply for them.

Future Business Leaders of America (FBLA). One of the clubs in high schools that I have seen with the most access to scholarships is Future Business Leaders of America. Students in this club can go on the Internet and apply for dozens of scholarships.

Military Scholarships. High School JROTC cadets do well when applying for military scholarships, if they want to go into the military after college. If your high school offers this class it is highly recommended that you take it because not only do you get some military experience, this experience counts when you apply for ROTC scholarships. The bottom line is that students who want to go into the military do themselves a lot of good by taking the high school military class.

Here is an example. Last year in our Gulf Breeze High School JROTC unit, we had six seniors (**pictured above**) apply for either ROTC scholarships or Academy appointments, and all six won. We had two win Air Force ROTC scholarships, two win Marine Corps ROTC scholarships, and one person win an appointment to West Point and one to the Air Force Academy.

When applying for an ROTC scholarship, it is especially powerful to be able to say that you held one of the highest JROTC leadership positions and the unit did extremely well.

This holds true with the other clubs in high school as well. The president of FBLA is usually competitive for lots of scholarships. So **my advice** is to try to find a club that is aligned with what you want to do in life, like FBLA or JROTC, join it and rise in its ranks. That effort may lead you to a scholarship.

Looking Locally. Another source of scholarships is also close to home. You may not even realize it but your parents' companies, the club you belong to, or the church you go to may offer some sort of scholarship. Search your organizations' and affiliations' websites or call them and ask.

Newspapers. I see scholarships and grants advertised in the local newspapers all the time. They are either asking for students to apply or getting some publicity while awarding the scholarship. Local civic groups like the Rotary Club and the Optimist Club award scholarships, and several others do as well. In fact, parents sometimes join a civic organization in hopes that their child will win one of its scholarships.

Accessing the Worldwide Web. The next thing you can do, and I **highly recommend** this, is to get on the Internet and look up college scholarships. I've mentioned above to do Internet searches on specific sites, but you should also do more comprehensive searches. For example, fastweb.com and cappex.com have search services to help find a scholarship you qualify for. This is how my daughter found the Best Buy scholarship.

Others sites I have seen are scholarshipexperts.com and scholarshipamerica.com. I do not recommend paying for a service. I am confident that you can find what you are looking for without having to pay for it.

You will find scholarship resources at coca-colascholars.org and thesalliemaefund.org. The Voice of Democracy Audio Essay Scholarship is found at vfw.org, and the Girls Going Places Scholarship at guardianlife.com.

A scholarship for my Florida resident students. Florida residents are eligible for the Bright Futures Scholarship. For the latest information, go to floridastudentfinancialaid.org. This scholarship has been a moving target as of late, probably because it has been costing the state so much to run that they have made it harder to obtain in order to lower their costs.

The Bright Futures Scholarship has worked out well for both of my daughters, but the requirements have risen since they won them. You will have to look up what the latest qualification test scores are.

At Gulf Breeze High School, they do a good job of getting everyone signed up and applying for it, but once given the ball you must run with it. There are community service requirements that can be easily obtained and documented, but, again, you have to make the effort to do so.

You must complete the **Free Application for Federal Student Aid** (FAFSA) to receive this scholarship. This is run by the U.S. Department of Education, and it requires that you enter a lot of your personal tax information into the form. They use this to determine your "financial need" score. This score will not affect your Bright Futures Scholarship, but it does go to the financial office at your college, which uses it to evaluate your financial need for scholarships, grants and loans.

TIP: Don't be surprised. FAFSA is an annual requirement. Make sure you keep your PIN, login, and your tax information that you used to fill out your first FAFSA, you will need it to fill out the form again for your next academic year. You will not be able to get your scholarship monies (Bright Futures, etc...) without doing the FAFSA every single year. Another tip is to have your taxes done, or at least an estimate done, before you start the FAFSA.

TIP: After you win your scholarships, you might find yourself waiting at your mailbox for the check to come in. Scholarships disburse their monies differently. Some will send a check, but others send the money directly to the school. You will see it when you register for school and your tuition comes due. The school will pay your bills and then issue you a check for what is leftover. For example, my daughter had over $2,000 in scholarships. About $1,500 was sent to the school, and after Bright Futures paid most of the tuition, they issued my daughter a check for about $400 that she used to buy books. Remember, different schools have different rules, so when you win a scholarship or grant, first contact them to see how the monies will be disbursed. If it is to the school, call the school to see how and when the monies will be applied to your tuition and fees and if there is a payout for anything leftover.

The FAFSA has another benefit. Once you fill it out, you will know whether it is likely you will qualify for federal aid, loans and grants. If you can get a grant, **take it - it is free money**. Loans, however, must be repaid, so be wary. Look at what the interest rate is and when the interest rate kicks in. Some don't start until you graduate, while others start accumulating interest right away.

Remember that some scholarships are not four-year scholarships. If you are making the decision on what school to go because you have won, or been offered, a scholarship, be sure to inquire exactly what the scholarship will cover.

Happy hunting and remember: *never – never – give up!* Your odds go up the more scholarships you apply for.

FLORIDA STATE UNIVERSITY *vs* UNIVERSITY *of* FLORIDA
The author's youngest daughter, SAMANTHA, *visiting her sister,* KASEY, *playing softball at the University of Florida*

Chapter Twelve

WRAP-UP

Chapter Twelve
WRAP-UP

I know the process of picking the right college and winning scholarships is daunting, but I hope the previous pages gave you an action plan to make a list of schools to look at, then narrow them down to your final choice, and a place to start when looking to pay the bills.

If you simply don't know what you want to study or cannot put together the funds to pay for a university, then I suggest starting at the local community college and, if possible, staying at home to save money.

As soon as you have a clear idea of what or where you would like to study, start your research. If you have found the subject you want to study, research which schools offer that major. You can use the steps in this book to help you to create your list, narrow it down, and ultimately decide on your school whether you are entering as a freshman, sophomore or junior. The requirements are different if you are entering as a **transferring student**. For example, the last I heard, you cannot transfer to the University of Florida until you have completed two years at a community college or received your Associates Degree (two-year program). Call the school and ask what its transferring requirements are.

If you are one of those people who know even in high school that you want to be a doctor, lawyer, or a member of another profession that requires post-graduate work, remember to look ahead to the graduate school you would like to attend and make sure the undergraduate school you choose will help get you there.

If you are like many who will discover their passion only after they are deep into their undergraduate program, then use this book once you've graduated to begin the process of choosing your graduate school.

REMEMBER

+ Start your research early;

+ Start with a wide range of schools;

+ Make your table with questions; fill out as much as you can from online research *from the schools' sites*;

+ Contact the schools and confirm what you've found and fill in what you could not find;

+ Visit the schools – *find the right fit*;

+ Research scholarships, grants and financial aid – *start early and apply to many!*

College is a launching point, not only because of the degree you receive, but because of the people you meet who may become lifelong friends or valuable contacts in business. It can be and should be one of the best times in your life. Picking the right college and having money to pay for it can make all the difference.

Bonus Chapter

FOUR-YEAR PLAN OF ATTACK

Bonus Chapter
FOUR-YEAR PLAN OF ATTACK

One of the most popular requests that I get from students and parents is for a copy of my list of things to do to prepare to get selected to a top school. It is quite simple. (For those of you who have heard me speak, the below list is a bit different from my presentation, easier to use as a reference tool.) I hope it helps you.

My experience is that schools are looking for well-rounded candidates with strong college preparatory backgrounds. In other words, you need to take the most challenging classes that are offered, and you need to fill in the time you are not studying with community service, sports, and other activities that show an ability to act independently and cooperatively within a group, leadership qualities, and an earnest interest in the greater good.

FRESHMAN YEAR

Good grades start here. Develop good study habits. Ask for help when needed. Work on developing good study and time management skills.

Start thinking about what you might want to do in life and where you might like to go to college. Keep a college notebook with a section for each school that interests you and a section to record activities you participate in, events you attend, clubs and committees you are a member of, that you can refer to when you write your college applications or scholarship essays.

Sign up for the college preparatory track at school. Classes to include are:

✦ At least *one computer science class* so you are very comfortable with computers, programs, and how to do Internet research. (Also, practice your typing! It's hard enough to write a college term paper without having to search for the letters on the keyboard to type it!)

- *Four years of English* if you can. Advanced Placement (AP) and Honors Classes in English would be even better.

- At least *two years of a Foreign Language*.

- *Four years of Math*, up to and including Calculus if possible. Again, take the AP and Honors Classes if offered.

- *Four years of Science*, including Biology, Chemistry and Physics.

- *Four years of Social Science*, including History, Economics, Government and Behavioral Science, if offered. Again, take the AP and Honors classes if offered.

NOTE: I often get asked about the value of dual enrollment (taking college classes while in high school) and about being home-schooled. I think dual enrollment is valuable, but make sure you get no lower than a "B" in those classes. The bottom line with being home-schooled is that you must take and do well on the ACT or SAT, so there is a standardized measure the schools you apply to can use in deciding your admittance. Reflecting back on all the students I have interviewed, it seems like all the home-schoolers I met did well on the standardized tests.

Scouting: If you are working towards becoming an Eagle Scout (the highest rank attainable in the Boy Scouting program) or earning a Girl Scout Gold Award (the highest of special awards recognizing rank advancement), that is great. If you can, stay in the program at least until the end of your junior year or the beginning of your senior year so you can include your participation and any awards or special rankings in your applications.

Clubs and Community Events: Start getting involved in extracurricular activities. Look for ones that offer leadership opportunities.

Sports: Join a team, especially one that is competitive.

READ! If you don't read, start. If you are a reader, read more. One of the things I have learned is that the most successful college scholarship applications were written by students who read a lot. I cannot understate this! The students who are well read are more articulate, imaginative, and remarkably versatile when it comes to problem solving. **My recommendation** is simply to read; read books, newspapers, magazines; read poetry, nonfiction and fiction; read aloud; and if you can, try writing in the style of those pieces you like best. This will serve you throughout your schooling, your career, your life.

SOPHOMORE YEAR

Get the best grades you can!

Extracurricular Activities: These are critical. To put it bluntly, there are thousands of students who will have good grades. The difference will be in what else they did in school. NOTE: *Do not make this mistake.* It is *not the number of things* that you did, it is the *quality* of the things that you did. Don't just become a member of a club, make your mark.

Student Government: Run for an office.

Civic Opportunities: Work on a committee. Actively participate in a civic organization or club.

Special Interests: Develop what really interests you and take it to the next level. If it is drama you love, get involved in the school or community theater; if it is music, join a band or choral group – what the colleges will be looking for is your *active* participation and *your contributions* to that field.

Sports: If you are not playing sports, try out for a team. If you already do play a sport, try out for the varsity team. If you think you will be competitive for an athletic scholarship of some kind, now is the time to talk to your coach. You should probably already be on the varsity team and doing well.

Your College Notebook: Take it out and start in earnest to narrow or add to your list of colleges. If you add new colleges, be sure to start doing your research on them (create and start to fill in a new table for each).

Consider going to the college fair for fun. Bring your notebook (and extra pens and pencils) so you can add notes on the schools that interest you. Make sure your notebook has blank tables in case you learn of a new school you want to get information on.

Tests: Take the PSAT and/or the PLAN test to get an idea what the ACT and the SAT are all about. **It is good practice**.

Summer: Use it wisely. Get a job. Attend summer leadership workshops. Participate in activities that will help build your resume. Athletes should be playing summer ball and going to college camps.

JUNIOR YEAR

This is your biggest year! You are going to start applying for college in the spring and summer of this year. Get your best grades.

Noting Deadlines: Pay attention to what the seniors are doing. Note when they are applying for scholarships and for colleges so you are ready when it's your turn.

The Final Four: Try to pare down your list of colleges to the top three or four so you can send your ACT and SAT scores to them. NOTE: You can go to the website and submit them to another school later if needed.

Get More Information: Make an appointment to talk with your counselor in the guidance office at your school about college. Show them your list and ask them what it takes to get in those schools. Some schools communicate often with the counselors, and they will have some good information for you. Also, tell them about your financial condition and ask them to help you find scholarships. REMEMBER: You should verify all information with the university or college itself. You may ask, *Then why go to the counselor at all?* Because they may have a contact at the school who will be especially helpful or know of a scholarship or grant that you might not find.

Go to More Fairs! If a college fair comes up, go! Take your notebook with its list of questions. Fill out as much of the table as you can for each of your remaining schools.

The BIG Tests: Consider taking the ACT and the SAT in the fall and then again in the spring. Have the scores sent directly to the schools you are considering. Take both tests because they are different; you may do better on one than the other. Consider taking a prep class for the tests – it will let you know if you should get some tutoring. Remember, some schools superscore, so taking the test several times may be helpful.

Your List of Activities and Accomplishments: Take out your college notebook and review the section where you've been keeping track of all that you have participated in (organizations, clubs, events, sports) and honors or achievement awards you have earned, then start to write paragraphs incorporating various combinations, if not all, of them and expounding on a few. When you start to fill out your applications, you will find some of your paragraphs will better fit certain applications than others.

NOTE: Some schools and some scholarships start their application process in the spring of your junior year! The Air Force Academy and ROTC scholarship applications open in the spring. You can start working on them now. *If you are applying to one of the Academies, you must also be nominated by your U.S. Senator or Representative.* Go to their Internet pages during the spring of your junior year and find out what is required to win their nomination. Many of their deadlines are in September (the start of your senior year), so you need to start work now.

While some colleges open up their applications in the spring of your junior year, others will open them in that summer and make their admission decisions sometime around December through February. *Be ready!* NOTE: Some universities have limited housing on campus and determine housing by the date they receive your application.

Start Visiting Your Short-List of Colleges: If possible make appointments for tours (some schools' tours are not impromptu or regularly scheduled), and call a contact at the school to ask if you can speak with them in person during your visit.

Summer: Athletes should be playing ball and perhaps attending college sports camps. If you don't already have a job, get one. Work on improving your ACT/SAT scores if needed.

SENIOR YEAR

This is the final big push - do not lighten up now!

Money Money Money: Look for scholarship and grant opportunities all year long. Some guidance offices list scholarships that are available. Watch the local newspapers for opportunities as well. Go to the Internet. Apply for all that you are remotely qualified for.

Tests: If you haven't taken the ACT and the SAT, take them. If you have and think you can do better, take them again.

Visiting Colleges: If there are any colleges that you are considering and haven't seen yet, plan a trip – remember to check out when the best time to go is, whether you need to sign up for a tour, and if there is a school representative you can meet with while you are there!

Applications & Their Deadlines: Finish up applications for admissions, as well as scholarships and grants. Start early for each, so you have time to review them. Pay close attention to deadlines and meet them with lots of room to spare.

Bonus Chapter

INTERVIEWS & TIPS

Bonus Chapter
INTERVIEWS & TIPS

So much has been written about interviewing. Just go to the Internet with a simple "interviewing" search, and your screen will fill with links to the "most important things to know," what questions you should be prepared to answer, what you should wear, there's even one that will tell you where the planets should be when you interview. So what could I possibly add? Personal experience and seven years of seeing what ultimately works for the interviewee and scholarship applicant.

What kind of experience? As an Air Force Admissions Officer, I have interviewed hundreds of high school students for potential appointments to the United States Air Force Academy and for Air Force ROTC scholarships over the past seven years. In fact, I conducted about 70 interviews this past year. I have interviewed students from Alabama, Mississippi, Georgia and Florida. In addition, as a leader in the Air Force I have interviewed people for jobs and awards. I interviewed one-on-one and as a part of a board. I have also sat on review panels and selection boards where we reviewed the results of interviews. I have been schooled extensively on the Air Force Academy interview process and how it is to be used by the admissions board.

Before I list the tips, I'd like to share two examples…

Interview Example One: A BAD START

I do remember one young lady who started by being late. It was just a few minutes late and the traffic was a bit heavy, so we gave her the benefit of the doubt. This was a morning interview, and I decided we should meet in neutral territory, the local Starbucks, so she would feel comfortable and we could casually have a cup of coffee and conduct the interview.

I have seen people dressed in all sorts of ways for their interviews – some are well-dressed and others are very casual. Unfortunately, her appearance was less than casual. In fact, it looked like she had just rolled out of bed and threw on whatever was laying on the floor. Her hair was unkempt, and her jeans were dirty and torn.

After I waved, she came over and introduced herself. This did not bode well, either. She smiled, and immediately I was taken aback by the food caught in her teeth.

When I make the appointment for an interview, I tell the Air Force Academy candidates that I am their advocate. I send them my questions in advance and tell them to take their time and answer each of them as completely as possible. At the arranged meeting, we will go over the answers, and I will ask them to expound on them and other related topics so that I can write 50 powerful lines to the Admissions Board.

THE CHAPEL *at the* MARION MILITARY INSTITUTE (MMI) *in* ALABAMA
MMI *is an Air Force Academy Preparatory School*

I tell them to treat our meeting as if it were a job interview. I will review their resume and anything else they want to bring. I am going to work hard to make them look great to the Admissions Board, but I can't do that unless they give me the "ammo." I tell them to bring their parents so they can help us brainstorm. This is because 18-year-olds can typically tell me what they did in school, but often have a hard time explaining why they did it, or, more importantly, what the impact was. Sometimes their parents can be very insightful regarding this.

This young lady had not answered all the questions I sent her, and the resume she handed me was poorly executed. She chose not to bring her parents. The **bottom line** was she was not prepared for the interview. We cut it short and agreed that she could e-mail me things when she had them ready to go.

I don't want to leave you hanging. Things did end well for this young lady. She did follow up with me. I coached her on how to prepare. I told her that I was going to be blunt but if she did what I told her, she would have a good chance at a scholarship. When she went to interview for the ROTC scholarship, she was ready, and guess what? She did well and won a scholarship. Hooray for her! She was willing to fix what went wrong, and it all worked out for her.

Interview Example Two: ONE of the BEST INTERVIEWS

I have had many outstanding interviews over the years. They usually last a little over an hour and are fun to do. The students I have met are exceptional. For the most part, they came well-prepared and told me interesting stories about their lives. They were deeply involved in their community, often leading the organizations they belonged to. It has been an honor meeting them and telling their stories to the Admissions Board.

One young lady was genuinely effervescent. It was not a pretense, she was just that way. She struck me as a natural leader, and that is exactly what was confirmed as I conducted the interview. When the interview was over, I wanted to join the Air Force Academy.

First of all, she was on time, despite having to travel more than an hour to get to the Starbucks we agreed to meet at. In fact, when I arrived, and I usually get there early to get a cup of coffee and open up my computer to the interview page, she was already there with her parents in tow and ready to go. She had her interview questions laid out for me and everything else in a folder ready for my review. She had a pen and paper to take notes, and she looked professional and eager for the interview.

GRADUATION *at the* UNITED STATES AIR FORCE ACADEMY

Her parents were high ranking and were still on active duty. They were very gracious and stayed to the side, only speaking when one of us had a question or when something needed to be clarified.

This young lady was athletic, intelligent and a leader. She was exactly what the Academy is looking for, except that her ACT/SAT scores were below the mean. She was the athlete of the year at her school for two years in a row. One of her teams went to the state championship game and another team was brand-new. She helped to start it.

She also started a girls club at the school. She wrote the charter, the bylaws, and got it all approved by the Principal. She recruited girls to join, and then led the fundraising so they could go on their outings, which she led.

It was a girls' outdoor adventure club. They went camping, canoeing, zip-lining, hiking, biking and climbing. The best part was her self-stated reward: to see the girls gaining personal confidence and coming out of their shells.

I actually wrote to the Admissions Board "… to not let this one get away. We need ladies like this in our Air Force." She did get in, by the way.

GRADUATION *at* WEST POINT

NOW *for the* INTERVIEW TIPS

First, **_be prepared_**. Do not underdress for the interview. Remember, you can always dress down once you get there, but it is hard to dress up if you don't have what you need with you.

For example, if you arrive in coat and tie or in a dress with a sweater covering your shoulders, you can quickly take off the coat or the sweater if you think it appropriate. The **bottom line** on dress is, too much is better than too little. Most people doing an interview will appreciate the fact that you went to the trouble to dress up for the interview.

**Have your homework done**.   Resumes and letters of recommendation or introduction should be well written and look professional. _(One quick note to pass on to those writing your letters of recommendation:_ Give them your resume and ask that if they write on your qualifications and achievements, not to reiterate those already listed. Most interviewers will have the resume in front of them, so it is just repeating. Ask them to write about their personal experience with you, what makes you stand out. I like to hear about a student's character, especially when it's conveyed in an anecdote.)

Actually **anecdotes are key**, even in resumes. Rather than listing a bunch of stuff, tell the reader why it was important. For example, it is nice that you were the vice president of the National Honor Society and led two fundraisers. It means more if you were vice president and you found out one of your peers had an accident and his family needed help paying the bills, so you organized two car washes and donated over $1,000 to the family.

**Correct Contact Information**: Make sure the phone numbers you leave for people to contact you are working numbers. The same goes for e-mail addresses – only give ones that you check regularly. I can't tell you how frustrating having the wrong information can be.   I am trying to get you an appointment to the Air Force Academy that is worth over $400,000, but I can't get you to answer an e-mail because you don't look there often or it's overrun with spam so you have no idea my e-mail has arrived. Also, you might want to go ahead and make a new account if your current e-mail address starts with something like beachbabe34@...com or superdude@...com. A better address is first name dot last name @ whatever dot com.

**Be on-time.**   It's a great first step toward making a good first impression and shows the meeting is a priority to you.

**Cellphones – TURN THEM OFF!** You don't want to be telling a story or explaining something and lose your train of thought when your phone vibrates. Not only that, it's just rude.

92

THE AUTHOR CONDUCTING *an* INTERVIEW

During the interview, make good eye contact and don't look off into space when you are thinking of an answer; it looks like you are making up a story. Sit up straight and don't tap your fingers, click your pen or shake your leg endlessly. It looks like you are ready to go, bored, or really nervous. Most importantly, always tell the truth.

Take notes. You are finally at the interview. You are talking with the person who may make the final decision, or at least may have a huge influence on the outcome. They probably have something to say that is worth writing down. At the very least, it makes it look like you are interested if you take notes.

I cannot tell you how many times I have had to lend someone a pen and give them a piece of paper, or how many times I have had to repeat what I said so they can finally write it down. You don't score points with the interviewer when he has to do the work for you or you make him repeat himself over and over.

Practice. I offer my students practice interview sessions. Surprisingly, few take me up on the offer. Some have done well without the practice; others come back and tell me their horror stories: *"He asked me about my character, and I didn't even know where to start."* I would have told them that a good place to start is with your values. A good example is the Air Force's Core Values – Integrity First, Service Before Self, and Excellence In All We Do.

If you are going to a military-related interview, then look up the services' values. They are all posted on the Internet. Learn about the creeds, mores and mottos of the service (Army, Navy, Air Force) to which you are interviewing. Then think about and be ready to tell how your own ethics and principles align with them. This is not limited to the military. Civilian companies do this too, and so do universities. For example, I received my undergraduate degree at Florida State University, and its motto is "Vires, Artes, Mores." If you were interviewing for a scholarship there, you might want to know what that means and then be able to describe what it means to you.

The **bottom line** is you should sit down with someone and practice interviewing even if it is just going over your resume and practicing answering questions about it. This is better than nothing. Be ready with your answers to typical questions like "Why do you want this appointment, job, scholarship?" "What makes you the best candidate for this?"

Here is a pair of questions I use to separate the wheat from the chaff. "What are your two (sometimes I ask for three) best character traits and explain why?"

Then I ask, "What are your worst two?" (Sometimes I ask for three.) If you think about it, these are not easy to answer off the top of your head. Many get tripped up on the worst, and they will take the easy way out and say that they can't think of any. I will follow up and encourage them to answer. A good answer is "persistence." You can say, "I am so persistent; I just try and try to get the job done."

Another good answer is "integrity." For example: "I will always tell you the truth, and sometimes the truth hurts a little, but it does make us better in the long run."

Don't be surprised if someone asks you if you ever had been fired or let go from a job, or if you have ever failed at anything. Sometimes I get some really surprising answers, good ones where a great lesson was learned or sadly some that just sink the interviewee.

The **bottom line** is that preparation can be the key to a good interview.

APPLICATION TIPS *and* REMINDERS

<u>***Do not miss a deadline***</u>. As I mentioned in Chapter Eleven on timing, many schools will advertise that their application deadline is in February, but they announce their first round of who is being admitted in December. Most schools start their application process some time during the summer. Get it done then, and if you have to update ACT/SAT scores, you can do that later.

The military ROTC programs and the Academies are very, very strict with their deadlines. If it says the first of December, they mean it. Do not miss that cut-off date.

<u>***Air Force ROTC Scholarship Tip***</u>. This application deadline is advertised as the first of December, and it is. The problem is most of the time the first board is in December. So if you wait until the first to get in your application, you may miss that December board.

Can you imagine if thousands of applications all came in on the first of December? How would you ever get them all processed and ready for a board in a week? Remember, most of December is taken up by the holidays. I imagine the applications that are processed earlier (October, November) make the first board, and the later ones meet the next one. Keep this in mind.

THE UNIVERSITY CLUB *in* SAN FRANCISCO

BEST OF LUCK AND I HOPE YOU GRADUATE FROM A UNIVERSITY AND THEN
YOU CAN JOIN THE UNIVERSITY CLUB PICTURED ABOVE

ACKNOWLEDGEMENTS

This book would not be possible if it were not for my family and friends who have helped me throughout the years. They brought me up, helped me along and pointed me in the right direction time and again.

Thanks to Mom and Dad for their unwavering, loving and caring support over the years. I would not be out and about helping others if it were not for them.

The same goes for Marie, my wife, and her family, and our daughters, Kasey and Samantha. Thanks for supporting me ... always.

Thanks to my brothers, Stan and Jim (and their families) for being great role models and helping me throughout the years.

Lastly, thanks to my friends, teachers and colleagues for their help, inspiration and friendship. Three friends and colleagues in particular helped substantially with this book and received no remuneration. Thank you for your generosity.

First is Mr. Steve Duckworth, who I acknowledged in the Forward as the inspiration for this book. Second, Mr. Joe C. Culpeper edited my original copy, sent me to the publisher, and coached me along the way. Lastly, Ms. Heather G. Wells proofread my second draft and made huge improvements in the text and the presentation of this book. Thanks to all of you.

CREDITS

Cover photos provided by Jason Thompson of the Gulf Breeze News, Gulf Breeze, FL

Photos listed in order of appearance:

1.   Fernandes, Michael, "The University of Notre Dame's Basillica of the Sacred Heart in the forefront as well as the Golden Dome in the background," Wikipedia Commons, 1 May 2012, Accessed 5 Jul 2013.

2.   Porsche997SSB, "Veterinary Education and Clinical Research at the University of Florida," Wikipedia Commons, 15 Apr 2011, Accessed, 5 Jul 2013.

3.   Miller, Robert Ward (Robertwardmiller), "Image of the University of South Alabama Jaguar Marching Band forming the 'USA' logo on the field at Ladd-Peebles Stadium in Mobile, AL," Wikipedia Commons, 15 Aug 2011, Accessed 5 Jul 2013.

4.   U.S. Department of Transportation, "U.S. Merchant Marine Academy Seal," En.Wikipedia. 5 Sep 2004, Accessed 5 Jul 2013.

5.   Spohpatuf, "Pugh Hall on the University of Florida Campus," Wikipedia Commons, 19 Jun 2008, Accessed 5 Jul 2013.

6.   Cholder68 of Flickr, "FSU vs Rice From the Sidelines," enWikipedia, 23 Sep 2006, Accessed 5 Jul 13.

7.   Author.

8.   Joel of Flickr, "5 Shot Panorama of Bryant-Denny Stadium at the University of Alabama During the 2009 A-day Game," Wikipedia Commons, 8 Apr 2009, Accessed 5 Jul 2013.

9.   Author.

10.   Author.

11. Fallowwell, Robby, "Nelson Hall," Wikipedia Commons, 25 Apr 2013, Accessed 5 Jul 2013.

12. Willmcc, "Fredric G. Levin College of Law at the University of Florida," Wikipedia Commons, 10 May 09, Accessed 5 Jul 2013.

13. Ahodges7, "United States Air Force Academy Cadet Chapel," Wikipedia Commons, 6 Nov 2009, Accessed 5 Jul 2013.

14. Author.

15. Author.

16. Author.

17. Milstead, www.ruralswalabama.org, "The Chapel at Marion Military Institute in Marion, Alabama," Wikipedia Commons, 8 Feb 2009, Accessed 5 Jul 2013.

18. Rogers, Dennis, U.S. Air Force Public Affairs, "Class of 2009," Wikipedia Commons, 27 May 2009, Accessed 5 Jul 2013.

19. Morrison, Jerry, MSgt, U.S. Air Force, "U.S. Military Academy Graduates," Wikipedia Commons, 23 May Accessed 5 Jul 2013.

20. Author.

21. Author.

Made in the USA
San Bernardino, CA
10 December 2013